The Heart
Of A Child

~

Praying About
the Things that
Really Matter

D0166969

Tom Lemler

The Heart Of a Child:
Praying About the Things that Really Matter

Tom Lemler
Impact Prayer Ministry
2730 S Ironwood Dr
South Bend IN 46614
www.impactprayerministry.com
tlemler@gapministry.com

When we read the words of Jesus that unless we become like little children we will not enter the kingdom of heaven, many of us struggle to know how to apply that in our lives. For me, a big part of living with the heart of a child is learning to pray with the faith and trust of a child.

This book is dedicated in grateful acknowledgment to God who has called me His child. It is also dedicated to my daughter, Susan, who teaches me much about living with the heart of a child. I thank the Deer Run congregation and my family — each of them helps me in a great way to pursue the calling and gifting God has put in my life. To all of these, and to you my readers, thank you!

Table of Contents

Some Things That Matter:

Introduction

How can my prayers for my children be more effective? What does God want for my child? What does God want for me as His child? What qualities should I grow in to become more like the child God created me to be? How would my prayer life change if I consistently approached God with the confidence of being His child? Through time in prayer, this devotional journal was written to help you understand, and live, some important traits of living and praying with the heart of a child.

You may use this book as a thirty-one day devotional or go through it at whatever pace suits you. Take your time to let each statement about the heart of a child sink deeply into your being. The book is designed to be used as both a devotional and a journal as you discover what God says about you.

Each topic follows the same three-page format. The first page is simply a statement of that day's focus and a scripture reference to get you started in God's Word. Look up the scripture reference and meditate on God's Word about the heart He desires for you.

The second page is some devotional writing that has come from my prayer time focused on that day's subject. It will include questions to help you think more clearly about what it looks like to have the heart of a child. There will also be some devotional thoughts to help you as you seek to grow in relationship with God. As you go through this page of each day's topic, spend time with God learning how to have a greater grasp of living with a child-like faith.

The third page is your turn to make this devotional even more personal! It contains a heading of the day's topic, some prayer points to help direct your prayers for a child of any age, and then a blank lined page. This is for you to record your interaction with God each day. Jot down your thoughts, your prayers, other scriptures that God brings to mind during your time with Him, and/or changes in your attitude or actions that He reveals you need to make. Use this journal page to help you remember and to help you grow.

In prayer,
Tom Lemler
Impact Prayer Ministry

Day One

Pray To
Be Directed
Toward God

(Genesis 18:18-19)

Directed Toward God

When do you find yourself most in need of direction? Who do you go to when you need direction? Why? Who are some of the people that have helped you along in your journey toward God? How have they helped? What direction have they given? What made their input credible? When you pray that someone would be directed toward God, are there ways that God might use you to be at least part of the answer to that prayer? How? Who are you praying for today that needs to be directed toward God?

As parents, it doesn't usually take long for us to start to realize just how much direction our children will need. And it isn't just the amount of direction needed that gets our attention, but the continuing nature of that direction often makes it appear that the need will never end. As we provide direction that promotes safety, education, manners, kindness, and so many other things, nothing is more important than our children being directed toward God. I ought to warn you though, when we pray for a child of any age to be directed toward God, He is most likely going to turn a mirror toward us and ask how our life directs people to Him.

Directed Toward God

As you pray for a child of any age, pray that they would be directed toward God. Pray for the courage and wisdom to be part of the directing process as God grants the opportunities. Pray to have a life that constantly seeks to be directed toward God so that you would be more aware of the direction others need. Pray that you would follow accurate direction, according to God's Word, and that others would find their direction based in it as well.

_____

_____

_____

_____

_____

_____

_____

_____

_____

_____

_____

_____

_____

Day Two

Pray To Be

Recognized As

God's Gift

(Genesis 33:5)

God's Gift

What makes a gift most valuable to you; the item itself or the one who gave it? Why? Have you ever received something that you didn't want or didn't know what to do with, but later came to realize its value as you began to understand the purpose of the giver? Explain. Do you know a child of any age that feels less valuable than the people around them? Is that child sometimes you? Why? How does what others believe about you change what you believe about yourself? How would having people recognize that every child is a gift from God change the way children of any age see themselves?

I have a very valuable collection of items on my shelves and window sill at work. Yet, when my office was broken into several years ago, not one of those items were taken. It is not until I tell the stories behind each gift that others begin to understand the value of both the item and the giver. In a similar way, I believe it is not only important that every child recognizes that they are a gift from God, but that we are more deliberate in seeing the life of everyone, including our self, as a gift from God.

God's Gift

As you pray for a child of any age, ask God to help you see them as His gift. Pray that each person would see their life as a gift from God. Pray for the wisdom needed to help others see children as God's gift. Ask God to help the children you are praying for know that they are valuable to Him and that He has created them to be valuable to others. Pray that we would value one another based on the One who has given them rather than on what they can or cannot do.

_____

_____

_____

_____

_____

_____

_____

_____

_____

_____

_____

_____

_____

Day Three

Pray That You Would Know The Mighty Works Of God

(Exodus 12:24-28)

God's Mighty Works

What is the most spectacular thing you have ever witnessed? How often do you talk about it? Why? What is the most incredible thing God has done in your life? Who knows about it? How do they know? What have you learned from others about the mighty works of God? What have you experienced yourself? How are you sharing what you have learned with those of the next generation? Do the children around you believe in a mighty God? Does the child within you believe in a mighty God? Why? What would it take for you to be more deliberate in sharing about the mighty works of God with others?

Whether easily impressed or a skeptic at heart, most of us have difficulty in giving God credit for the mighty works He does in and around us each day. While unintentional, we often follow in the pattern of the Egyptians, and Israelites, who dismissed the early mighty works of God as irrelevant. While the mightiest work of God in our life is being saved from eternal death by the blood of Jesus, there are many other works being done by Him that we ought to also be sharing.

God's Mighty Works

As you pray for a child of any age, ask God to help them be aware of the mighty works He has done, and is doing, in their life. Pray for eyes that can see the mighty works God is doing in your life. Pray for wisdom in sharing with children about the mighty works of God. Pray that your testimony about God's mighty works would help the children around you know of God's desire and ability to save them. Pray that the child within you would reflect the mighty work God has done.

_____

_____

_____

_____

_____

_____

_____

_____

_____

_____

_____

_____

_____

Day Four

Pray That Life Would Go Well

(Deuteronomy 4:40)

A Life That Goes Well

Has your definition of what "life going well" looks like changed over time? In what way? Why? What is the most important part of living a life that goes well? Why? Are you more focused on helping children get what they want or on finding what they need to live a good life? Why? What's the difference? What does obedience to God have to do with a life that goes well? Does your level of obedience serve as a good example to the next generation? How has your obedience, or lack of it, impacted the people around you? Would you be more obedient if you were to realize how much doing so helps life to go well for others? Why?

I suspect that we all want a life that goes well for the children around us and for the child within us. Praying that it goes well is a great start, but our obedience to God is where our prayers are put into action in this matter. While it can be easy to focus on the stuff that this world offers, Jesus asked, "What does it profit a man to gain the whole world but lose his soul?". Praying that life goes well means that we are asking God to help a person live in obedience so their soul is not lost.

A Life That Goes Well

As you pray for a child of any age, ask God to help you pray from a position of obedience. Pray that God would give you an eternal perspective to what is needed for life to truly go well. Pray that you would practice a life of obedience that helps life to go well for the child in you and for those children around you. Pray for hearts of understanding in you and in the children you pray for, so each of you would know God's perspective of what a life that goes well looks like.

_____

_____

_____

_____

_____

_____

_____

_____

_____

_____

_____

_____

Day Five

Pray That You Would Know God's Commands

(Deuteronomy 6:4-9)

Know The Commands of God

Have you ever not done something you should have because you didn't know you were supposed to? How do you feel when you miss opportunities that you should have known about? Are there times you have done something that you didn't know was wrong until after the fact? How did you feel? Did you wish someone had warned you ahead of time? Why? How diligent are you about learning what God wants and expects? Do you feel responsible to help others know the commands of God? Why? How does your comfort level in living and talking about the commands of God help others to know them?

Years ago I was pulled over by the police for committing a driving infraction when I wasn't aware I was doing anything wrong. After the policeman gave me a written warning, a person riding with me said, "Oh, yeah, you can't do that in this town." My immediate thought was, "That would have been nice to know before I drove through the town rather than after." Our willingness to talk about God's commands, and practice them, in all situations will go a long way toward our children knowing them.

Know The Commands of God

As you pray for a child of any age, ask God to help you be more aware of His commands. Pray for help in expressing the suitability of His commands in all situations. Pray that the children around you, and the child within you, would know the commands of God as tools meant to help you and not to harm you. Pray for wisdom in living and sharing the commands of God with people who have not yet chosen to follow them. Pray that your obedience to the commands of God would help the next generation know their value.

_____

_____

_____

_____

_____

_____

_____

_____

_____

_____

_____

_____

Day Six

Pray That You Would Return To God Whenever You Stray

(Deuteronomy 30:1-3)

Return To God

Have you ever been lost or found it necessary to be away from familiar surroundings for an extended period of time? How did you feel? Why? Are there times when you begin to doubt if you could ever return to a place, or person, you once valued? Why? What does it take to return to a relationship you once rejected? How does your forgiveness of children, and yourself, help each of you to know you can return to God even after you stray? Are there people that you think are too far from God to ever return? What does God say? How does your return to God when you stray give hope to those watching you?

Many people, including children, find themselves estranged from one another and from God. Sometimes the separation is so great, or the reasons so personal, that we begin to think there is no way back. One of the most beautiful promises in the Bible is the promise of God that He will be found from wherever we are when we seek Him with our whole heart. There may be no message more powerful that we can communicate to our children than the message that there is always a way home.

Return To God

As you pray for a child of any age, ask God to help you remember your journey to Him, including the times you have strayed and returned. Pray that the children around you, and the child within you, would live in the humility that allows for a full reconciliation of those who stray. Pray for a softening and removal of pride which keeps the wandering child from believing they can return to God. Pray for a practice, and acceptance, of forgiveness which can bring about a restoration once thought impossible.

_____

_____

_____

_____

_____

_____

_____

_____

_____

_____

_____

Day Seven

Pray That You Would Know The Joy of The Lord

(Nehemiah 12:43)

Joy of The Lord

How joyful are you? Would your closest friends agree? Would strangers agree? Why? What is the source of your joy? Does your level of joy vary? Why? How does living with the joy of the Lord change the amount of joy you express in your day to day life? What does the joy of the Lord mean to you? How can you help others to find and have it? What is it about your relationship with the Lord that brings you the most joy? How often do you express that reason, and that joy, to others? Do you think the children around you, and the child within you, believe you have great joy in the Lord? Why?

Living with joy is not easy, especially when much of what we label as joy is based upon the circumstances of life being in our favor. The joy of the Lord, however, tends to be based upon two things. One, a recognition of the Lord's presence with us, and two, an understanding of what the Lord has done for us that only He could have done. When we help the children around us understand those two things, we set them on a path where the joy of the Lord can be found. When the joy of the Lord is in us, there will be no hiding it.

Joy of The Lord

As you pray for a child of any age, ask God to fill you with a joy that can only come from Him. Pray that your expressions of joy will help the children in your life to know that true joy can be found when we seek it in the Lord. Pray for wisdom in leading others to see a path of joy when the journey they are walking is filled with difficulty. Pray that you would be an example to the children around you when it comes to ways to express the joy the Lord has filled you with.

_____

_____

_____

_____

_____

_____

_____

_____

_____

_____

_____

_____

_____

Day Eight

Pray That You Would Offer A Life of Praise To God

(Psalm 8:2)

Offer Praise To God

How do you feel when people praise you? Is that feeling different based on why they are praising you or what you perceive their motives to be? Why? How often do you praise others? Why do you praise them? Do you think they appreciate it? Why? What would it look like if your praise of God would come from a child-like heart? Would it sound different? Would its source be from a different reason? How does your giving, and accepting, of praise help children learn to offer praise to God?

Praise is an interesting thing because we tend to use it in our interactions with one another in ways that aren't always pure. One of the big differences between praise and flattery is the motive behind what we say. True praise, and particularly our praise of God, should always be about Him because making it about what we want isn't really praise. When we live a life of honest praise, we teach our children that we value God, and them, simply for who they are. The praise that comes from children, and from the child within us, is a praise of innocence that exalts God and silences those opposed to Him.

Offer Praise To God

As you pray for a child of any age, ask God to help each of you offer praise which is genuine. Pray that your example of praise would lead others to honor God with their words and their life. Pray for honesty in examining the motives behind the praise that is expressed. Pray that the heart of a child would always be turned toward God in praise. Pray that each person would learn to offer praise to God simply because they value His presence in their life.

_____

_____

_____

_____

_____

_____

_____

_____

_____

_____

_____

_____

_____

Day Nine

Pray That You Would Know The Fear Of The Lord

(Psalm 34:11)

Know The Fear of the Lord

Is fear a good thing or a bad thing? Explain. What does "the fear of the Lord" mean to you? Why? How do you feel about fearing the Lord? Why? What are some things that a good and healthy fear protects you from? What are some things that an unhealthy fear has kept you from? What's the difference? How does learning and practicing a healthy fear lead to greater wisdom? What have you learned about having a fear of the Lord that you wish you had learned earlier? How does that help you to pray for others to know the fear of the Lord?

As an emotion, fear is a very complicated thing. As a decision, however, fear can be a choice that leads us down a path of good and right choices. When you pray for a child of any age to know a fear of the Lord, you are asking God to direct them in a way of wisdom. This is a fear that understands both the consequences of disobedience and the love of a forgiving Father. When we live with a fear of the Lord, we help others to see the joy of walking in obedience — not just to avoid the "wrath of God", but to honor the Father who loves us beyond measure.

Know the Fear of the Lord

As you pray for a child of any age, ask God to help them know the fear of the Lord as a good and positive thing. Pray that they would find wisdom in following a path outlined by a godly fear of the Lord. Pray that God's love would change those who feel more terror than fear. Pray that your life would help others to know that there is joy to be found when you fear the Lord according to the honor that He deserves. Pray that those around you would choose obedience which honors God.

_____

_____

_____

_____

_____

_____

_____

_____

_____

_____

_____

_____

_____

Day Ten

Pray That You Would Know A Compassionate Father

(Psalm 103:13)

Compassion Of a Father

In your mind, how well do the words father and compassion go together? Why? Have you experienced compassion from an earthly father? How does that influence your view of compassion from God? Why do you need compassion? Why do you need to show compassion? When you are suffering for any reason, how comforting is it to have someone who understands the pain you feel? How does the compassion you show others help them to believe more fully in a Father who longs to be compassionate toward them? How does God's compassion temper His judgment?

Compassion is one of the qualities that flow from the Father to those who fear Him. It is His understanding of our suffering, and His suffering with us, that keeps the fear we ought to have from becoming a terrifying thing. When a child of any age suffers, it is a comforting thing for them to know the compassion of a loving Father. As those who represent the nature of God to others, we have the privilege of not only receiving that compassion, but also of sharing it with so many others who suffer in this life.

Compassion Of a Father

As you pray for a child of any age, ask God to make His compassion obvious to them. Pray that they would know that they do not suffer alone. Pray for wisdom in how God would have you share in their suffering. Pray for those whose fathers on earth have not been the examples of compassion that they should have been. Pray that the compassion received from a heavenly Father would lead to our having compassion for one another.

_____

_____

_____

_____

_____

_____

_____

_____

_____

_____

_____

_____

_____

Day Eleven

Pray That You Would Live With Pure And Right Conduct

(Proverbs 20:11)

Pure and Right Conduct

How do you decide what is pure and right? Why? Would your typical actions make others believe you are one who seeks to do what is pure and right? Why? How difficult is it to choose pure and right conduct all the time? Does a person's reputation require perfection in all of their actions? Why? Do your expectations of others exceed that of your own conduct? Why? When you think about a child of any age, how much help do they need to maintain appropriate conduct? Who do they need that help from? Who do you need help from in order to live pure and right?

It seems that every generation gets tagged with a label based on the perceived conduct of those who garner the most attention. Few of us like labels that are inaccurate — especially if the inaccuracies paint us in a negative way. On the other hand, none of us are perfect, so how we are viewed will always be based on what is most visible in our life. Our influence in the lives of others will generally lead them further into, or further away from, pure and right conduct. Looking for the good in others will not only make it more visible to us, it will make it more desirable to them.

39

Pure and Right Conduct

As you pray for a child of any age, ask God to fill them with a desire to do what is right and pure in His eyes. Pray that you would live as an example to those around you. Pray that you would not expect perfection but would look for the pure and right conduct in others in order to nurture it. Pray that the view of pure and right that you seek and share would always be based on what God says. Pray that the children around you, and the child within you, would always be known for pure and right conduct.

_____

_____

_____

_____

_____

_____

_____

_____

_____

_____

_____

_____

Day Twelve

Pray That You Would Follow Proper Training

(Proverbs 22:6)

Follow Proper Training

What are you good at? How did you get that way? How do you feel about training? Why? Have you ever thought you were good at something and then discovered there was a better way of doing it than what you had been taught? How did you feel? Have you ever had to learn something you thought you would never use but later found it to be a very useful lesson? How did your attitude about the earlier training change? How involved are you in training others for the future.

At the heart of any training is a process that rarely produces immediate results. We train in order to become better at a particular skill set and we train others so that they would know how to do, or be, something that they currently are not. But it is not just important that we train or provide training. No, it is critical that the training we seek and pray about is proper in the eyes of God. Practicing a skill incorrectly will not help us improve; it only serves to solidify a less effective means. When we train a child of any age in the way they should go, we must be certain the instruction and training are based on the Word of God.

Follow Proper Training

As you pray for a child of any age, ask God to help them follow proper training. Pray that they would learn to appreciate the instruction that comes from God's Word. Pray that you would be equipped to provide proper training because of the training you yourself follow. Pray that you would not lose heart when those around you do not appear to be responding to the training they receive — at least not in the time frame you think is appropriate.

_____

_____

_____

_____

_____

_____

_____

_____

_____

_____

_____

_____

_____

Day Thirteen

Pray That You Would Know The Correction of Godly Discipline

(Proverbs 22:15, 23:13, & 29:15)

Correction of Godly Discipline

What are your thoughts on discipline? Why? Do you think more often of punishment or correction when you hear the word discipline? Why? Is there a way that all three of those practices work together? How? How does godly discipline relate to spiritual training? Is there a difference in how you view discipline based on if you are giving or receiving it? Should there be? Why? Are there areas of your life where a lack of discipline has made you less effective than you could be? What are you doing about it?

Discipline is a practice we rarely like when it is applied to us, yet we can be quick to see how others would benefit from it. It is our own acceptance of discipline that does the most to help others learn the value of it in their life. While we like to separate out the pieces to avoid what we find to be unpleasant, godly discipline involves both punishment and correction. When done well, punishment makes us aware of the consequences of our actions, correction teaches us the new course of action we should take, and discipline carries us through the process of putting those new actions into practice.

Correction of Godly Discipline

As you pray for a child of any age, ask God to help them know and accept the correction of godly discipline. Pray for a heart that is willing to learn the fruits of discipline. Pray that your involvement in disciplining others would be done in humility and love. Pray that you would know, and help others to know, the truth of God disciplining those He loves. Pray for an understanding of proper punishment and correction so that godly discipline can happen.

_____

_____

_____

_____

_____

_____

_____

_____

_____

_____

_____

_____

_____

Day Fourteen

Pray That You Would Know God's Faithfulness

(Isaiah 38:19)

The Faithfulness of God

Who is the most faithful person you know? What makes them that way? Have you ever changed your opinion of how faithful someone was? Why? Do you believe in God's faithfulness? What specific things have influenced your level of belief? Are there things that you do that would help or hinder the view others have of the faithfulness of God? What? Who did you learn about faithfulness from? Who is learning about faithfulness from you? What are they learning?

In a world where promises are often broken without thought, it can be difficult for a child of any age to grasp the absolute faithfulness of God. Experience with people has taught us to be skeptical and just because someone kept their word once, it doesn't mean they will keep it again. That is why the telling of our stories of God's faithfulness in our life is so critical. We need reminded, and the children around us need reminded, that God has been faithful in our past and His nature, along with our experience, will teach us about His continued faithfulness. Your story of God's faithfulness needs to be shared and heard.

The Faithfulness of God

As you pray for a child of any age, ask God that they would always know of His faithfulness. Pray that you would find ways to share the lessons you have learned of God's faithfulness. Pray that God would help you to be a more faithful person so that the children around you would have a visible example of what faithfulness looks like. Pray for the courage to tell your stories of God's faithfulness. Pray that God would help you to learn from the testimonies of others.

_____

_____

_____

_____

_____

_____

_____

_____

_____

_____

_____

_____

_____

Day Fifteen

Pray That You Would Be Brought Near To God

(Isaiah 43:5-7)

Brought Near To God

Who in your life do you feel closest to? Why? What factors brought the two of you to that point of nearness in your relationship? Were there other people who helped? How? When you think of your relationship with God, how close would you say you are with Him? Why? What has brought you to that point? Have people helped you to draw near to God or have they made you feel more distant from Him? How? Knowing that God longs to draw His children near to Himself, how does your life express that longing of God to the children around you?

While physical proximity can help, feeling near to someone usually has more to do with a connection of the heart than a joining of hands. God says that when we draw near to Him, He will draw near to us. As we share the love of God with a child of any age, we tell of His desire to draw them near. Being wanted goes a long ways toward building the bonds of closeness and no one is wanted more fully than we are wanted by God. His desire for the children around us, and for the child within us, is that each of us would be brought near to Him and find a closeness like no other.

Brought Near To God

As you pray for a child of any age, ask God to help them know His love for them. Pray that each child would be brought nearer to God as they see the example of your closeness with Him. Pray that your desire would always be for a closeness with God that no one could separate you from. Pray that each child would know they are wanted by God even if they feel unwanted by everyone else. Pray for the courage to live in such a way that no child would ever believe they are unwanted.

_____

_____

_____

_____

_____

_____

_____

_____

_____

_____

_____

_____

_____

Day Sixteen

Pray That You Would Know Peace

(Isaiah 54:13)

Know Peace

What is peace? How much of it do you have? Why? What is the source of your peace? Explain. When is it most difficult for you to feel at peace? When do you most need to know peace? Are those two times related? How? Does peace mean that all conflict has been removed from your life? Explain. What role does the teaching from God's Word have in helping you experience peace in the midst of conflict? Does your usual demeanor help others experience peace? Why? How does the peaceful demeanor of others help you to know peace in difficult circumstances?

Since Jesus said we would have trouble in this world, I have to believe the peace He promises is something different than simply a lack of conflict. In fact, He tends to shine most brightly in our life when we learn to live with His peace in the midst of the difficulties we find ourselves in. If we want to help others know real peace, we must begin with accurate teaching from God's Word. But it is not enough to simply teach it, we must live it in such a way that the children around us would know what true peace is because they can see it in us as we live for Christ.

Know Peace

As you pray for a child of any age, ask God to help them know the peace that can only come from Him. Pray that they would see that peace lived out in your life as you trust God in the midst of conflict. Pray that your accuracy in sharing the truth of God's Word would lead to a greater peace in your life and in the lives of those around you. Pray that you would seek to end and resolve all conflict even as you live with peace in the midst of it.

_____

_____

_____

_____

_____

_____

_____

_____

_____

_____

_____

_____

_____

Day Seventeen

Pray That You Would Be Comforted

(Isaiah 66:13)

Know God's Comfort

Are there times when you have been comforted? When? What worked? Have you ever not been comforted by the efforts of someone who was trying to comfort you? Why? What things make a person's efforts to comfort you seem real? Why? Is compassion related to comfort? How? Does a person's experience in situations similar to yours help you to accept the comfort they offer? Why? How does the comfort offered by a person differ from the comfort that God can give? In what ways are they the same? How does the experience of God's comfort give you hope as you pray for a child of any age to be comforted?

We live in a world filled with loss of many kinds. It is in the midst of loss, even perceived loss, that we find the need to be comforted. An uncomforted child of any age can quickly become an angry, confused, and/or hurt person that acts out in ways that are often inappropriate. When we experience sadness, God desires that we come to Him for comfort so that we would be able to comfort others with the same comfort that we have received from Him.

Know God's Comfort

As you pray for a child of any age, pray that they would be open to receiving the comfort God desires for them. Pray that God would use you as an instrument of His comfort in the lives of others. Pray for the courage to look to God for comfort that exceeds the comfort the world can offer. Pray that the comfort you receive from God through His Spirit and/or through people He sends your way, would equip you to share comfort with others.

_____

_____

_____

_____

_____

_____

_____

_____

_____

_____

_____

_____

_____

Day Eighteen

Pray That You Would Have Hope For The Future

(Jeremiah 31:17)

Hope For The Future

How do you feel when you think about your own future? Does that answer change based on the length of time you define "future" as being? Why? When you think of the future that the children of today will face, how hopeful are you? Why? What role does faith have in your level of hope? What is it that you're really asking God to provide when you pray that a child of any age would have hope for the future? How can you be more involved in helping others see Jesus as the only real hope for both now and the future?

Hope seems to be one of those words that either has great meaning or no meaning depending on how we define it. Some of our "hopes" are no more than wishful thinking and we know it. But when we place our hope in the promises of God, we find a confidence in the future that comes through faith in a God who views eternity as easily as we view a single moment. It is in Christ that hope for the future exists. That means a huge part of our prayers regarding hope for the future must center on people living in relationship with Jesus. It is this hope that not only helps us now, but prepares us for eternity.

Hope For The Future

As you pray for a child of any age, pray that they would know a hope that is more than wishful thinking. Pray that they would allow God to open their heart and mind to the wider view of eternity that allows them to see beyond today's struggles. Pray that your hope would be centered with confidence in the promises of God so that your message of hope to others would be believable. Ask God to help each person you are praying for cling to an everlasting hope that cannot be taken away.

_____

_____

_____

_____

_____

_____

_____

_____

_____

_____

_____

_____

Day Nineteen

Pray That You Would Know The Goodness Of God's Gifts

(Matthew 7:11)

God's Good Gifts

What is the best gift you have ever received from a person? What is the best gift you have ever given to someone? What makes a gift "good"? Have you always received what you have asked? Why? Have you ever received something better than what you asked for? Did you recognize it as better immediately, or did it take time to learn the real value of the gift? How does love influence the gifts you give and receive? When love is the motive, are the gifts you give and receive more about what is wanted or what is best? Why?

Some of the greatest gifts I have received did not seem that great at first glance. As I look back on life, I realize I have learned to trust the goodness of God's gifts, even when I don't understand them, because I had parents who gave of themselves out of love. We didn't have everything that others had, and there were times when I didn't think what I had been given measured up, but I generally understood (eventually) that the gifts given to me were both good and for my good. God makes it clear that whatever ability we have to give good gifts pales in comparison to His ability and desire to do so.

God's Good Gifts

As you pray for a child of any age, ask God to help them understand the absolute goodness of His gifts. Pray that you would know the goodness of God so you can share of that goodness with others. Pray that God's love would be expressed by you in the way you love others. Pray that you would give of your best as you represent the goodness of God to the people around you. Pray for a heart of understanding when the goodness of God's gifts take time to recognize.

_____

_____

_____

_____

_____

_____

_____

_____

_____

_____

_____

_____

_____

Day Twenty

Pray That You Would Understand The Things Of God

(*Matthew 11:25*)

Understand The Things of God

What are some things that you find difficult to understand that seem easy for others? How about things that are easy for you yet others struggle with? Why? Have you ever been in a group where it seems everyone except you understands something that is going on? How did it feel? How do you feel when you learn a "secret" that opens up a pathway to greater understanding? Are you likely to share that knowledge with someone else who is struggling to understand the same thing, or keep it to yourself? Why?

In my hobby of wildlife photography, it is often someone's willingness to reveal location information that leads me to be able to photograph a specific animal I am looking for. Most of the time, though, that information only comes when I admit I don't know everything and ask for help. I suspect it is an element of pride that keeps the things of God hidden from the "wise and learned" even as those things are revealed to those with the faith of a child. When we trust the "inside information" that comes from God's Word and His Spirit, we open our hearts to a greater understanding of the things of God.

Understand The Things of God

As you pray for a child of any age, ask that God would help them have a greater understanding of His kingdom and righteousness. Pray that they would be open to God revealing Himself in ways they understand. Pray for the humility to go to God with the child-like faith He requires. Pray for an understanding of the things of God that would exceed that of those who think themselves to be wise. Pray that you would be generous in sharing with others about all that God has revealed.

Day Twenty - One

Pray That You Would Enter God's Kingdom

(Matthew 18:2-3)

Enter God's Kingdom

What is the most exclusive place or event you have been to? Were there requirements or expectations you had to follow in order to gain access? What would have happened if you had chosen not to accept the conditions of entrance? What makes humility so valuable when you approach situations that are above what you know you deserve? Do you think children are more likely than adults to freely accept gifts they know they haven't earned? Why? In what ways do you think we must become like children in order to enter the kingdom of God? Why?

Entering an exclusive event or location usually requires at least two things — an invitation and an agreement to abide by certain expectations set forth by the host. There is good news when it comes to entering God's kingdom; He has issued the invitation to "whosoever will" and made it possible through Christ for anyone to meet the requirements of entrance. In fact, the expectations are easy enough to grasp, that God tells us we must become like little children in order to have the humility necessary for entrance into His kingdom.

Enter God's Kingdom

As you pray for a child of any age, ask God to help them know how welcomed they are in His kingdom. Pray that no one would view God's kingdom as being out of reach for them. Pray for the humility to become like a little child so that you may enter the kingdom of God. Pray that you would be welcoming in the way you interact with children so they would grow in their sense of belonging. Pray that you would always be truthful about the simplicity of God's invitation.

_____

_____

_____

_____

_____

_____

_____

_____

_____

_____

_____

_____

Day Twenty-Two

Pray That Your Approach To God Would Not Be Hindered

(Matthew 19:13-15)

Approach God Unhindered

Have you accomplished every thing you had hoped to by this stage in your life? Why, or why not? What are some hindrances that either stopped you or seemed insurmountable at the time? How does the attitude of people around you influence your willingness, and even ability, to press on when things become difficult? Does the level of that influence change based on who the person is? In what ways? Are there ways your words or example may be hindering a child from approaching Jesus, or even wanting to? What will you do about it?

As a child of any age, we all have people we look up to that likely have more influence on us than they even know. Likewise, there are people looking to each of us as examples, and how we represent Jesus will either encourage or hinder them from seeking Him. Our words, both in content and tone, can either lift someone up and point them to Christ or knock them down with such discouragement they feel they have no hope. God's desire is that we would build up and welcome one another so we would not become a hindrance to anyone's faith.

Approach God Unhindered

As you pray for a child of any age, ask God to remove anything that would become a hindrance to true faith. Pray that you would be an encourager of children as they seek to know God. Pray that you would examine anything in your life that has been a hindrance to you having the vibrant relationship with Christ that He desires. Pray that the lies of the enemy would be defeated so that you, and children of all ages, would know the value each person has to God.

Day Twenty-Three

Pray That You Would Live As God's Child

(John 1:12-13)

Live As God's Child

What are some values, qualities, expectations, or characteristics that represent the family you belong to? How well do you reflect them? Are there attributes that others see in your life that identify you as coming from a specific family? How would you describe God? What are His characteristics that you appreciate the most? What are some benefits that you normally expect to experience as part of a family . . . especially as a child in that family? What does living as God's child mean to you in terms of both responsibility and privileges? Why?

Like it or not, people that know your parents tend to have certain expectations of you based on whose child you are. When we claim God as our Father, people who know God, and even those who don't, have certain expectations of what a child of God should live like. But it is not just people. As you read God's Word you find He has set forth the standard for how a child of God ought to live. Living as God's child gives us a combination of great responsibility and great privilege. When people observe how we live, there ought to be a family resemblance to our Father.

75

Live As God's Child

As you pray for a child of any age, ask God to assure them of their value as His Child. Pray that you would live as a godly example of what a child of God should look like. Pray for the humility to lead others toward a life that seeks to imitate Jesus in both attitude and action. Pray that each child would know the joy of living as the child of a Father who loves them beyond measure. Pray that God's presence would be seen in each of His children, including you.

_____

_____

_____

_____

_____

_____

_____

_____

_____

_____

_____

_____

Day Twenty-Four

Pray That You Would Respond To The Call of God

(Acts 2:38-39)

Respond To God's Calling

Are there certain invitations that you are more likely to accept than others? Why? What makes an invitation "acceptance worthy" to you? Have you ever been invited to an event that you knew was way above what you deserved? How did the invitation make you feel? Did you accept it? When you have an open invitation to bring others with you, do you? Why? How much do you want others to enjoy the best things you have been able to experience in life? How has responding to God's calling impacted your desire for others to know Him?

I have had opportunity to do ministry with people that I felt were way ahead of me in just about every way possible. Being invited to join them was both a great privilege and very humbling. Many times when we share God's calling of people to Himself, the initial response may be one of unworthiness. Yet God makes it clear that His invitation and promises are for everyone, the "whosoever" part of John 3:16! As we work and interact with children of all ages, our presentation of the gospel with our words and life ought to lead them to respond to God's call.

Respond To God's Calling

As you pray for a child of any age, ask God to help them recognize, and respond to, His calling. Pray that you would understand the wonder of God calling people to Himself. Pray for the humility needed to respond to a calling you don't deserve. Pray about how you will be involved in helping children know that God's calling is for them. Pray that your response to God's calling would be shared with the children around you, even as the child within you accepts it.

Day Twenty-Five

Pray That You
Would Grow Up
And Put Away
Childish Ways

(1 Corinthians 13:11)

Put Away Childish Ways

When was the last time someone told you to grow up? Why? What is the difference between childish ways and child-like actions? Is the difference more about the action or the attitude? Explain. How does the normal growth from infancy to maturity relate to what should happen after we are born into God's family? What are some things that keep people from growing up? Are there things you hold on to that God would view as childish? What are they? What should you do about it? What will you do?

We typically don't fault an infant for crying when it is hungry or in need of something. We understand, and hopefully teach better responses, when they take what they want with no regard for others. However, when they carry that type of behavior into adolescence and beyond, we consider the selfishness to be very childish. When God instructs us to put away our childish ways, the starting place is usually with our attitudes. When we replace the childish attitudes of selfishness and entitlement with the child-like attitudes of sharing and generosity, we find the child within us grows toward maturity.

Put Away Childish Ways

As you pray for a child of any age, ask God to give you patience with them and an understanding of their process of growth. Pray that the childish things in their life, and yours, would be identified so they can be put away. Pray for wisdom in knowing how to keep a child-like faith while putting aside childish ways. Pray for a spirit that longs for a maturity that seeks the good of others. Pray for the humility necessary to both change and gently guide others to growth.

_____

_____

_____

_____

_____

_____

_____

_____

_____

_____

_____

_____

_____

Day Twenty - Six

Pray That You Would Imitate God

(Ephesians 5: 1)

Imitate God

Have you ever visited the reenactment of an event or seen a replica of a historical item? Why would a person do that? Have you ever tried to imitate someone? Why? Were you successful? What makes you want to imitate someone? Does the level of someone's love for you influence how much you want to be like them? Why? Do the people closest to you ever say you look, act, and/or sound just like your parents? Are they right? If you could choose one characteristic of your life that you would want others to imitate, what would it be? Why?

The value of the reenactment of an event, or replica of an item, in learning about the real thing is dependent on the accuracy of the imitation. As His children, God calls us to imitate Him because not only is it good for us, doing so is what allows the people around us to see Him in us. When we encourage the children around us, and the child within us, to imitate God, we show the world whose child we really are. It is God's immense love, demonstrated through His Son, Jesus, that ought to motivate us to be filled with a great desire to imitate Him.

Imitate God

As you pray for a child of any age, ask God to fill them with a desire to imitate Him. Pray that you would be a student of God's Word where He reveals Himself through its pages, as well as through His Son and His Spirit. Pray that you would live a life worth imitating as those watching you see Jesus represented well. Pray for a spirit of discernment that leads you to imitate the things of God you see in a person rather than simply imitating that person.

Day Twenty-Seven

Pray That You Would Live As Children Of Light

(Ephesians 5:8-9)

Children of Light

What things do you typically associate with light? How about with darkness? Why? Which do you prefer? Why? Do you know children who are afraid of the dark? Are you one of those children? What things help to dispel, or at least lessen, that fear? Do you always want light to expose everything that is hidden? Why? Does being reminded that the light will always expose things hidden by darkness influence the choices you make when it appears no one is watching? Why? How does God's love make being exposed by His light a desired thing?

Many children are afraid of the dark because it hides the reality of a safe environment, and may even contain unseen dangers. When we live as children of the light, we allow God's light to assure us of the safety He provides and to reveal to us the dangers of the world we live in. Even while the light may expose our sin, we can be confident that God's love is great enough to offer forgiveness and restoration when we turn to Him. Choosing to walk in the light not only helps us to see where we are going, that choice serves to remind us that we don't walk this life alone.

Children of Light

As you pray for a child of any age, ask God to help them pursue a life that is lived in the light of His Word. Pray that you would trust God enough to seek His light both for clarity and correction. Pray that you would know true freedom from living in the light and that you would apply that freedom to those who need to move from darkness into light. Pray for the courage to change when God's light exposes that need. Pray for humility as you shine God's light without condemnation.

_____

_____

_____

_____

_____

_____

_____

_____

_____

_____

_____

_____

_____

Day Twenty-Eight

Pray That You Would Live Obediently

(Ephesians 6:1, Colossians 3:20)

Live Obediently

How obedient are you? Why? Would the people who spend the most time with you agree? Why? What level of obedience do you expect from others? Does it differ depending on who the "others" are? Why? How much disobedience to you find acceptable in your own life? In the lives of others? How does knowing that something is right affect your desire to do it? Why? How does love change your desire to be obedient to someone? Does it change how you view the disobedience of someone? How?

Life is filled with rules, laws, and instructions that each of us have to choose our level of obedience to. Often our expectations of obedience by others exceeds our own practice of obeying. As Christians, we expect children to obey their parents because God says so but our lifestyle may not always reflect our obedience to God even though He calls all of His children to the same obedience. Fear of punishment can be a motivation to obey, but God's expectation is that we would be obedient because it is the right thing to do for people who love Him. When we obey because it is right, we help others learn obedience.

Live Obediently

As you pray for a child of any age, ask God to help you evaluate your own level of obedience. Pray for the humility needed to model an obedient life that others can see. Pray that your love for God would compel you to do what is right. Pray that God's practice of forgiveness would be your example when the children (of any age) around you fail in obedience. Pray for the courage to do what is right, and lead others in that direction, even when it seems no one else does.

_____

_____

_____

_____

_____

_____

_____

_____

_____

_____

_____

_____

_____

Day Twenty-Nine

Pray That You Would Know Genuine Love

(1 John 3:18)

Know Genuine Love

How do you know if someone loves you? If someone says they love you but they don't act like it, do you believe them? Why? What does genuine love look like? What is your criteria for the answer given? In what ways has God expressed His love for you? Do you believe Him? Why? Do you think the children (of any age) around you believe you love them? Why? When you have been corrected, by people or by God, has that been done in ways that you knew you were still loved? How? How will you love others in a way that they will know it to be genuine?

It seems that words only go so far when it comes to expressing love. We can say it all we want, but if our actions do not show love to others they will soon doubt our words. Children seem to be especially vulnerable as they try to determine if our words are true. Training up a child in the way they should go will generally require a good amount of correction. God's training and discipline of His children is always done in the context of His love. When our service and sacrifice for others remains visible in the midst of correction, we help them know genuine love.

Know Genuine Love

As you pray for a child of any age, ask God to help you know the depth of His love for you and for them. Pray that you would learn to love others with deeds and actions, in addition to words. Pray that you would pay attention to God's discipline of you so you would know how to love others even in the midst of necessary correction. Pray for the courage to love fully, just as Christ has loved you. Pray for eyes that would see those who feel unloved and then pray for the wisdom to love them with the genuine love of Christ.

_____

_____

_____

_____

_____

_____

_____

_____

_____

_____

_____

Day Thirty

Pray That You Would Know The Greatness Of God

(1 John 4:4)

Know God's Greatness

What makes a person great in the eyes of the world? In your eyes? In God's eyes? What ways are those responses similar or different? Why? Do you believe greatness comes from a person's physical body or from something inside them? Explain. Has your view of what makes a person great changed from when you were a child? In what ways? Have others ever considered you greater than you view yourself? What do they see that you don't? How will knowing God's greatness, and seeing it in His children, change the way you live?

Ask most people what makes a person great and you will likely receive as many answers as the number of people you ask. Some view greatness based on physical, mental, or even social ability. Others see it as a product of the influence you have on people. God actually defines His view of greatness when He says, "Whoever would be greatest of all must become servant of all." When God's Spirit lives within us, not only should we recognize the greatness of God but we ought to be exhibiting that greatness as we serve others. When we view God from the eyes of His child, we find the greatness that we need.

Know God's Greatness

As you pray for a child of any age, ask God to help you recognize His greatness dwelling within people. Pray for the courage to understand greatness from God's perspective. Pray that you would be an example to the children around you as you live in God's greatness by serving others. Pray for the humility to serve God, and serve people, when the world wants to convince you that you ought to be served by others. Pray for a child-like heart that can see the greatness of God.

_____

_____

_____

_____

_____

_____

_____

_____

_____

_____

_____

_____

_____

Day Thirty - One

Pray That You Would Walk In The Truth

(2 John 1:4, 3 John 1:4)

Walk In The Truth

How do you determine what is true? Is there a difference between knowing what is true and walking in the truth? Explain. How truthful are you? Would the people who know you the best agree? Would God agree? Why? How much effort do you put into pursuing truth? Does your pursuit of truth inspire others to seek God's truth? How do you feel when those you have instructed no longer live in the way they were taught? Why? Does your life bring joy to the people who shared the truth of God with you?

In a culture that seems to thrive on half-truths, deceptions, and straight out lies, choosing to walk in the truth can be a very lonely path. As children of God, His desire is that we would not only know His truth, but that we would apply it and live it in everything we do. Our adherence to the truth of God's Word sets an example that those being born into Christ will take notice of. Just as we want people to accept the instruction we give them, we rob God of joy when we choose to not walk in the truth that He has given. Our greatest joy can be had when we see people walking in truth because of our example.

99

Walk In The Truth

As you pray for a child of any age, ask God to help you examine how diligently you pursue His truth. Pray for the courage to proclaim Jesus as "the way, the truth, and the life" in a world that rejects absolute truth. Pray that your obedience to the truth would bring joy to those you have learned from. Pray that the children around you would learn of God's truth from both your words and your actions. Pray that you would be filled with joy as you see children walking in the truth.

_____

_____

_____

_____

_____

_____

_____

_____

_____

_____

_____

_____

Bonus Day

Pray That You

Would Learn

A Lifestyle

Of Prayer

(Luke 11:1)

Lifestyle Of Prayer

How do you view prayer? How much is prayer a part of your life? Are there things that you don't pray about? Why? Does prayer feel as natural to you as breathing? If not, why not? Do you ever feel that the prayers of someone else are more effective than yours? Why? In a healthy relationship, what do little children tend to talk about? Would becoming "like a little child" before God change the way you pray? In what ways? Who could you learn from about prayer? Who could you teach about a lifestyle of prayer?

If children trust you, they will often volunteer information that you may not even want to know. Their honesty and transparency comes from a pure heart that hasn't been taught there are some things you just don't talk about. It is that heart that I go to when I want to learn, and teach, about prayer. Somewhere along the line, many of us have been taught proper discretion in our conversations with others and somehow we have applied that to the things we will talk to God about. A lifestyle of prayer recognizes that nothing is hidden from God and frees us to be in communication with Him about everything.

Lifestyle Of Prayer

As you pray for a child of any age, ask God to help them know His understanding of whatever is on their mind. Pray that He would help you to examine yourself for anything you've been afraid to talk with Him about. Pray that He would increase your desire to build your relationship with Him through the conversation we call prayer. Pray that God would surround you with people that you can learn from, and that you can instruct, in a lifestyle of prayer.

_____

_____

_____

_____

_____

_____

_____

_____

_____

_____

_____

_____

Made in the USA
Columbia, SC
17 September 2019